D0313305

BRENT LIBRARIES

Please return/renew this item
by the last date shown.
Books may also be renewed by
phone or online.
Tel: 0115 929 3388
On-line www.brent.gov.uk/libraryservice

OXFORD
UNIVERSITY PRESS

Previously ...

In the story *Message in an X-bot*, Max has a strange little robot that needs repairing.

Max asks Ant for help. Together they fix the robot.

The robot comes alive! It plays them a message – a hologram. A woman tells the children to *"beware of Dr X!"*

Ant keeps the robot as a pet. He calls it Rover.

Chapter 1 – A robot spy

"Don't look now," said Cat. "But I think we're being watched."

Cat was with Max, Ant and Tiger in the park. She pointed at a nearby tree.

Slowly, each of the boys turned round and looked up. They saw a small green robot sitting on a branch. It was trying to stay hidden behind some leaves, but it was staring right at them.

"It looks just like Rover ..." whispered Ant. He pulled his pet robot from his pocket. "Except Rover is red."

"That probably means it comes from the same place," said Tiger.

"You're right," said Max. "We should try and catch it."

Max spoke very quietly. He told his friends to surround the tree. When everyone was in place, Max reached up towards the robot. But it was no good. The robot had seen them. It gave a loud *BLEEP!* Then it ran down the trunk of the tree and quickly scuttled away.

"After it!" Max cried. "Don't let it escape!"

The children chased the robot across the park. Max reached out to try and grab it … but the robot suddenly picked up speed. It shot off along the path and plunged into a drain with a *SPLASH!*

"Blast!" said Max. "We'll have to shrink and follow it."

"No way," said Cat. "It's far too dark down there."

"We can take my micro-torch," said Max. "And Tiger's got a light on his watch. Come on, it'll be OK!"

"Are you sure?" cried Tiger. "We could meet anything down there, like rats and sp ... sp ... spiders."

"Great," said Ant, excited. "We should definitely go, then."

"See, Ant thinks it's a good idea," said Max. "Come on, Tiger, don't tell me you're scared!"

Tiger didn't like spiders when he was BIGGER than them. Down there and micro-size ... he shuddered at the thought.

Chapter 2 – Going underground

Max fished inside his backpack for his torch.
He found some string, too.

"OK, is everybody ready?" said Max.

They turned the dials on their watches.

They pushed the X and …

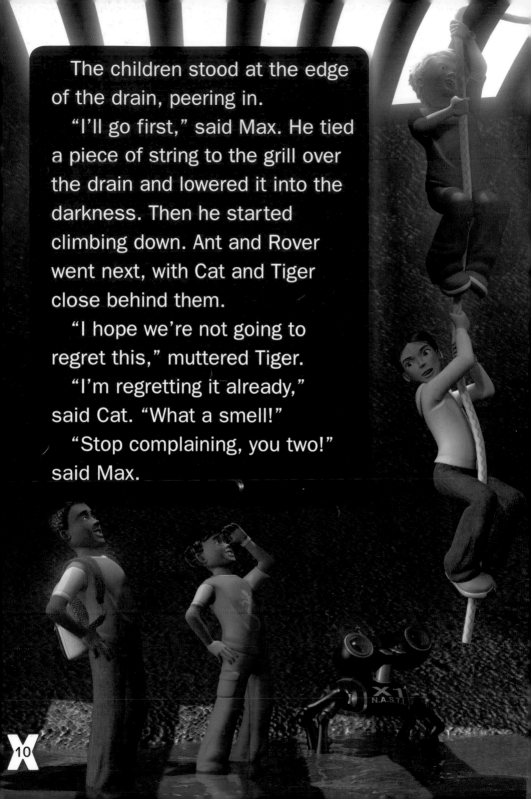

The children stood at the edge of the drain, peering in.

"I'll go first," said Max. He tied a piece of string to the grill over the drain and lowered it into the darkness. Then he started climbing down. Ant and Rover went next, with Cat and Tiger close behind them.

"I hope we're not going to regret this," muttered Tiger.

"I'm regretting it already," said Cat. "What a smell!"

"Stop complaining, you two!" said Max.

They had reached the bottom of the drain. In front of them was a large puddle of dirty, smelly water. On the far side of the puddle, there was the entrance to a tunnel.

"Hey, look at these marks," said Max, shining his torch into the tunnel. "The robot must have gone down there. Let's follow it."

Max strode off, sweeping the torch in front of him and keeping his eyes on the floor.

"Ugh, what's that?" said Tiger as something long wriggled past.

Ant felt it, too. "It's probably some kind of centipede," he said. "Shine your watch-light on it and I'll tell you what kind."

"Er … don't worry," said Tiger. "I don't really want to know."

The tunnel went deeper. The micro-friends had to cross a narrow piece of wood over a deep crack in the ground. The roots of plants and trees were tangled above them. There were also lots of pipes and cables around them. They had to move carefully. Rover began to bleep quietly. He was only a robot but he seemed nervous.

Then there was a pale greenish glow ahead of them. Suddenly, Max stopped.

"Oh, wow!" he gasped. "I don't believe it …"

The robot's trail had come to an end. So had the tunnel. The micro-friends were stood in some sort of pipe at the end of the tunnel. In front of them was an underground room full of giant computer screens.

14

On one side of the room was a huge screen with the word NASTI written on it. Standing at the control panel in front of the screen was a strange-looking man in a purple suit.

"Be careful ..." whispered Cat. "We'd better not let them see us."

"Cat's right," said Max. They stepped back into the shadows.

"What is this place?" said Tiger. "It's like something in a movie."

"I don't know," said Ant. "But look, there's the robot!"

The micro-friends watched as the robot
scuttled up to the strange-looking man.
The man bent down, picked up the robot and
plugged it into a control panel. What happened
next gave the children a nasty surprise ...

A series of pictures started to appear on the huge screen – pictures of them! The robot must have taken them. It must have been spying on them!

Another picture appeared, too. It was somebody they recognized.

"Hey, that's the lady we saw in the hologram that Rover played to us!" cried Tiger. " I wonder who she is?"

 Suddenly, Rover started to bleep in alarm. *BLEEP! BLEEP! BLEEP!* Everybody in the room turned and stared ...

Chapter 4 – The chase in the dark

The strange-looking man pointed towards the children. He yelled something about "X-bots" and "watches". Then he hit a big red button on the control panel in front of him. An alarm instantly sounded … *WHOOP! WHOOP! WHOOP!*

Small doors opened in the walls of the huge room. Hundreds of green robots poured out. They scuttled across the floor and headed straight towards the children.

"I told you coming down here was a bad idea ..." said Tiger.

"And you've never, ever had a bad idea, have you Tiger?" snapped Max.

"Stop arguing," said Cat. "We don't have time."

"Er ... I agree," said Ant. "Let's just ... RUN!"

The children ran as fast as they could through the dark tunnels, but the robots were getting closer and closer. They buzzed and they hummed and their legs clicked and clacked. The sounds echoed in the tunnels.

"We're not going to make it!" cried Cat, glancing over her shoulder.

Max knew that this was his fault. He was the one who had persuaded the others to follow the robot in the first place. Now they were in real danger and it was up to him to save them. But how?

Cat, Ant and Tiger ran across the narrow piece of wood that crossed the deep crack in the ground. But just as Max reached it, the wood collapsed. He was stranded.

Chapter 5 – A desperate leap

"Max!" cried Cat.

Quickly, Max took some string out of his backpack and threw one end over a tree root above his head. He tied it firmly and waited.

"What are you doing?" yelled Tiger.

"Keep running!" called Max. He could hear the robots clicking and clacking down the tunnel. "I'll catch you up!"

Max could see the robots coming. Their eyes glowed red in the darkness as they streamed towards him. Max waited till the very last second ...

He grabbed the string, jumped and swung across the hole. The robots clattered down into the deep crack. They bleeped and squeaked. Then he heard them splash into the water far below.

"Way to go, Max!" cried Tiger, giving him a high five.

The others hadn't kept running. They needed to know Max was safe.

"Let's get out of here," said Max.

"That's the best idea you've had all day," Cat laughed.

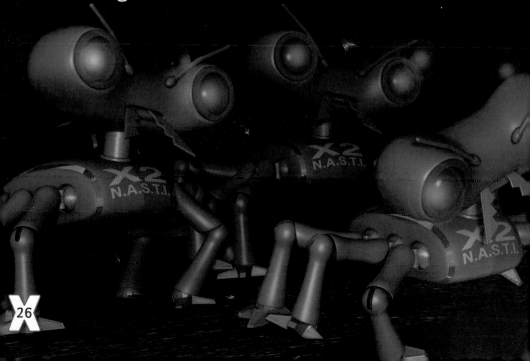

Later, back in their micro-den, the children talked about what they had seen. They had lots of questions.

WHO? QUESTIONS:

Who is the strange-looking man in the purple suit?

Who is the lady in the hologram?

WHAT? QUESTIONS:

What is the strange-looking man up to?

What are all those robots for?

What are X-bots?

What is NASTI?

WHY? QUESTIONS:

Why are there pictures of us on the screen?

Why did the robots chase us?

Max, Cat, Ant and Tiger weren't sure they wanted to know the answers, but they all knew one thing. It had something to do with their watches!

NICE

- NICE = National Institute for the Creation of Energy

- Mission = To create clean energy to power the city

N.I.C.E.

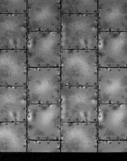

NASTI

- NASTI = Nano Science and Technology Inc

- Mission = Unknown (but definitely not nice!)

Find out more ...

For more underground adventures read ...

The Knockits of Knockity Hoo

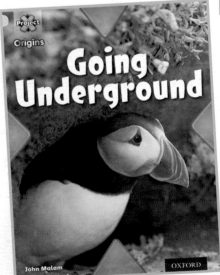

Going Underground